How to Avoid Collisions

The Inland and International Rules of the Road Made Simple

By the same author

The Captain's Guide to Liferaft Survival

How to Avoid Collisions

The Inland and International
Rules of the Road Made Simple

Captain
MICHAEL CARGAL
Master Mariner

SHERIDAN HOUSE

This book is dedicated to
Captain William Evans,
of the British Royal Navy,
who first thought of putting red and green lights
in the rigging of ships,
so they wouldn't run into each other.

Copyright © 1991 by Michael Cargal
First published 1991 by
Sheridan House Inc.,
Dobbs Ferry, NY 10522

Library of Congress Cataloging-in-Publication Data

Cargal, Michael, 1946-
    How to avoid collisions : the inland and international rules of
the road made simple / Michael Cargal.
        p.   cm.
    ISBN 0-924486-16-3 : $17.95
    1. Collisions at sea. 2. Rules of the road at sea. 3. Ships-
-Safety regulations.   I. Title.
JX4434.C37   1991   91-22377
341.7'5666—dc20   CIP

Printed in the United States of America

CONTENTS

ABOUT THIS BOOK

The Rules of the Road are easy to understand but hard to learn. The Rules themselves make sense, and the reasoning behind each Rule is clear; however, as a group the Rules are complicated. They were drafted with the help of lawyers and written in lawyerese.

The key to understanding and remembering them is to see through the wording and into the meaning. Much of this book is the Rules of the Road rule by rule but not word for word. I have translated the lawyerese into plain English and rearranged the information into what seemed to me more logical groupings.

When I quote or paraphrase the rules, I use this typeface.
When I comment on the rules, I use this typeface.

All of the information from the Rules that a captain needs to know to run a boat is included in this book, but I have left out some details, such as the vertical and horizontal spacing of lights. You would need to know these things if you were building or refitting a boat, but you don't need to know them to run one. I have also rounded off some numbers. For example, 20 meters is 65.6 feet, but I round that off to 65 feet.

I have done my best to convey the exact meaning of every Rule, but if you need the exact wording of a Rule, get publication CG-169.

INTRODUCTION

Followed correctly, the Rules of the Road keep boats from running into each other, and every captain and watchstander should know them well.

History

England enacted the first steering rules in 1846, requiring vessels to pass port to port, because ships were colliding in the English Channel when one captain didn't know what another intended to do. The new steamships were faster than sailing ships, so there was less time to correct misjudgment.

Two years later red and green sidelights and a white masthead light were required for steamships. Fog signals were added in 1858.

Other countries, including the United States, adopted their own rules. France and Great Britain agreed on the first International Rules in 1863. The United States got together with other seafaring nations in 1889 and agreed on uniform international rules.

The Rules Today

As experience and technology have advanced, the Rules have been changed and expanded.

Now the Rules divide vessels into classes according to how easily one can get out of another's way. They specify lights, day shapes, and horn signals so everyone knows which class a particular vessel belongs to, what direction it is going, and what it intends to do.

They even take into account the fact that in bad visibility you might 'see' on radar someone who doesn't see you.

And they specify a standard of responsible seamanship regarding lookouts, risks, and factors for the captain to consider in navigation.

Jurisdiction

The Rules of the Road have the force of American law for any vessel in U.S. waters and for any American-flag vessel anywhere in international waters.

The International Rules are the same anywhere in the world in international waters, but governments are allowed to make special rules for their own inland waters, which means harbors, lakes, and rivers. The U.S. has done that. Captains of boats over 12 meters (39 feet) in inland waters are required to have a copy of the Inland Rules on board.

The U.S. Inland Rules are almost the same as the International Rules. The differences will be pointed out as we go along. There are also a few special rules for the Great Lakes and western rivers, which will be mentioned at the appropriate place.

Canadian Rules

International Rules apply in all Canadian waters, but Canada has made a few additions, either to clarify ambiguous Rules or to conform to U.S. Rules in the Great Lakes and Western Rivers.

SECTION 1

Standards of Seamanship

Before describing who has the right of way and what lights and day shapes must be shown, the Rules set a standard of responsible seamanship for a captain, or other watchstander, and give rules for some special situations.

Sometimes these standards of behavior are specific and detailed, but they are frequently very general, saying only that you are required to know what is safe and you are required to do it. In every case, the Rules deal only with preventing collisions. Other aspects of seamanship are important, but they are outside the scope of the Rules.

The spirit of the Rules is clearest in Rule 2, Responsibility, which combines the Rule of Good Seamanship and the General Prudential Rule from the old Rules of the Road.

RESPONSIBILITY

The Basic Rule

Nothing in these Rules can excuse you if you cause a collision by not following the Rules, or by not taking some precaution which your particular case requires or which is the ordinary practice of seamen.

Courts are unforgiving about collisions. You are required to know the Rules of the Road, and you are required to follow them. If you don't follow some Rule, and you cause a collision because you don't, you can't use any other part of the Rules to weasel out of it. You can't hide from the Rules, and you can't hide behind them.

Departing from the Rules when Necessary

In following these Rules, you must take into account any danger of navigation and collision and any special circumstances, including the limitations of the vessels involved, which might make it necessary to depart from the Rules in order to avoid immediate danger.

You mustn't follow the Rules blindly. You have to be alert and aware. If the circumstances of the case make it unsafe to follow a Rule, you must break that Rule that one time.

Special circumstances that might make it dangerous to follow the Rules include:

- the limitations of the vessels
- more than two vessels approaching each other
- doubt as to the intentions of the other vessel
- a nearby hazard to navigation, such as shallow water or a reef

These special circumstances are reasons to depart from the rules only if following the Rule would cause immediate danger. Inconvenience is not an excuse. The Rules are important, and they should be followed.

LOOKOUT

The Basic Rule

You must maintain a proper lookout at all times, by every means available and appropriate at the time, specifically including sight and hearing, so you can make a full appraisal of the situation and of the risk of collision.

These Rules are only about preventing collisions. It's a good idea to keep a lookout to avoid hitting a reef, but you **must** keep a lookout to avoid hitting another boat.

On ships, a designated lookout must stay as low and forward as possible (for better visibility in fog) and may have no other job at the time than lookout. On boats, the watchstander must pay attention all the time.

Using Radar

This Rule means you have to use your radar at night or whenever the visibility is bad. It doesn't mean you have to have a radar, or that it has to work, but if you have a working radar, you must use it at night, or in reduced visibility, so you can know if another boat is out there farther than you can see it in the darkness, so you can assess the risk of collision.

Does it mean you have to keep your radar on in good daytime visibility? Not exactly. But if your radar is turned off when you hit someone, the presumption in real-world courts will be that you weren't using every means you had available to make a full appraisal, because radar plotting would have told you the speed and course of the vessel that ran into you, and if you had known that you might have avoided the accident.

The same thing is true if you had your eyes glued to the radar, and you didn't see the little boat you ran over because it was a bad radar target. You are required to look and listen, too. This means that at night on a trip along a deserted coast, you still have to keep the bridge lights turned off. It means you can't play music on the bridge so loud you can't hear another vessel's horn signals or someone calling you on the VHF. How loud is that? There is no objective standard, but if you don't hear a horn and then have an accident, any music you had on was too loud.

SAFE SPEED

The Basic Rule

You must always go at a safe speed so you can take proper and effective action to avoid collision and be stopped within a distance appropriate to the situation.

How Fast is Safe?

You must always go slow enough that you can always turn quickly enough or stop short enough not to hit someone. How fast that is depends on your boat and the circumstances.

In bad visibility, you must also be able to stop at least within half the distance you can see. If both boats can do that, and if they see each other and take action immediately, they won't collide. If the other boat doesn't see you right away or is going too fast to stop in its half of the distance, you'll hope your own boat has some stopping and turning left in it.

Factors to Take into Account

The Rules can't say exactly how fast is safe, but they do say you must take certain things into account when you, as captain or watchstander, decide how fast to go.

All vessels must take into account:

- *the visibility*
- *the traffic density, including concentrations of fishing vessels*
- *how well your vessel handles*
- *how short you can stop in the prevailing conditions*
- *shore lights which might mask or be confused with another vessel's lights, or a buoy, or backscatter from your own lights*
- *the wind, sea, and current*
- *how close you are to danger*
- *your draft compared to the water depth*

**In addition, if you have radar, and if it is working,
you must take into account:**

- *your particular radar*
- *how good it was when it was new*
- *its present condition*
- *the range you are using*
- *the fact that the sea, weather, and other things can sometimes
  return false echoes or hide real ones*
- *the fact that some things don't reflect radar waves well,
  such as logs, ice, and small boats*
- *the number, location, and movement of vessels you see on your
  radar*
- *the more exact assessment of the visibility that may be possible
  when radar is used to determine the range of vessels or other
  objects in the vicinity*

RISK OF COLLISION
The Basic Rule

You must use every appropriate means to determine if there is any risk of collision.

This Rule repeats that you are required to look out of the windows, to listen for horn signals and listen to the radio, to use radar if you have it, and to pay attention all the time. The broad language is meant to include rapid radar plotting and auto-plotters.

What if You're Not Sure?

If you have any doubt whether there is risk of collision, you must assume that there is.

Requirement to Use Radar Properly

If you have a working radar, you must use it properly. You must use the long ranges enough to know that another boat is out there early enough to avoid it.

You need the information in time to use it. Modern container ships may cruise at 20 or 25 knots. If you keep your radar on 3-mile or 6-mile range to make sure you don't miss a small boat, you may not see someone big and fast until it's too late to avoid a close-quarters situation.
    And it is not enough just to see a target on the radar:

Requirement for Systematic Observation on Radar

You must do radar plotting or equivalent systematic observation of radar targets.

The Risk of Collision Rule specifies the bare minimum for radar observation.

First, put your bearing marker on the target.

If the target stays on the bearing marker, you must assume there is risk of collision.

Tug   Barge

If the target goes off the line, there still might be risk of collision, particularly when approaching a large vessel, or a tow, or a vessel at close range.

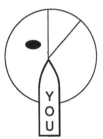

Assumptions Based on Limited Information

You must not make assumptions on the basis of scanty information, especially scanty radar information.

The Rules point this out because radar gives you only relative motion, unless you plot or have a gyro-stabilized north-up radar. You can't tell from any radar screen whether you are looking at the stern of a target or the side.

Sometimes it's hard to pick the targets out of the clutter in the center of the screen. And just because you don't see it on radar doesn't mean it isn't there.

RADAR PLOTTING

Except for making all the right horn signals in Newport Harbor, the requirement for systematic radar observation is probably the hardest part of the Rules of the Road for a boat to follow exactly, although the plotting itself is easy.

Rapid radar plotting is a technique for quickly determining the speed and course of a radar target. In six minutes you know how close you're going to come to the target and what direction you have to turn or how much you have to slow down to avoid coming too close to it. It's a wonderful set of tricks, and the Coast Guard wisely requires merchant marine officers to learn it.

Autoplotters

Ships over 10,000 tons all have automatic radar plotters, but most boats don't. On those boats that do have them, they can be useful in smooth seas but are generally useless in moderate to heavy seas, especially in a smaller boat, because boats can yaw so much that the automatic plotting ends up as a fluorescent smear rather than a clear line, as the targets jitter over 20 or 30 degrees of screen. One swipe of the coastline's echo can wipe out a quadrant of targets.

Reflector Screens

Non-automatic plotting is also often impractical. The Rule was written for ships. In addition to autoplotters, ships have reflector screens on their radars, clear-orange sheets of plastic that cover the screens and bend upward at the edges. Using a reflector screen is like drawing on the inside of a shallow, luminous bowl. You draw on the plastic with a white or yellow grease-pencil, and it looks as if you're drawing on the radar screen. You mark the position of a target, note the time, draw a couple of lines with your grease-pencil and ruler, and one tenth of an hour later (6 minutes), you know how to avoid hitting the target. It's simpler than it sounds, and it's kind of fun. Unfortunately, real-world boats don't have radars with reflecting screens. I've worked on boats since 1964, and I've never seen one outside the testing room.

Paper Plotting

The Coast Guard's answer is for you to plot on paper. You can buy paper radar plotting sheets. You mark the targets' positions with a pencil. This works on merchant ships, where you have a seaman at the helm, a lookout in the bow, and an officer in charge of the watch. It doesn't work on a boat when you're the only one up at night.

Although the Coast Guard says you should always have two people on a watch, in the real world, boats under about 100 feet (and not carrying passengers for hire) seldom carry enough crew to have two people up all night, much less two to a bridge watch. The ordinary practice of seamen in that case is one to a night watch. Insurance companies, who are in the business of discouraging people from doing risky things, require only three crew on a boat going from San Diego to Cabo San Lucas. Three watchstanders can get enough sleep on that trip if they stay up one at a time, but they can't with two on a watch. A charter crew of two fishing albacore simply couldn't operate with both on night watch. Even larger boats carrying passengers for hire, who are supposed to have two crew on watch at night, have only one on the bridge, with the other as a roving deck watch.

If you're alone on the bridge during a night watch, and you see a radar target off your bow, turning on a light bright enough to work by, even a red one, might impair your night vision. And rapid radar plotting by pencil and paper takes more time than it does on a radar screen. There are many times day or night when you don't want to take your attention off the water ahead long enough to do the plotting. Many smaller boats don't even have chart tables. Few have them on the flying bridge, where the driver is likely to be when navigating in a high-traffic area. On a boat without an autopilot, it would be well nigh impossible.

The Answer

I think you sometimes have to declare rapid radar plotting impossible under the prevailing circumstances (and even dangerous, under Rule 2) and satisfy the spirit and the letter of the Rules by doing the closest thing you can, applying an abridged version of the radar plotting techniques as an 'equivalent systematic observation.'

Equivalent Systematic Observation

This presumes that you are the captain of a yacht. Your radar is relative motion, head up, with no reflector screen or automatic plotter. The console has enough bare space for a notepad but not a radar plotting sheet.

You are on night wheel watch along a deserted coast, with the radar set on 12-mile range. A deckhand checks with you from time to time, but basically you are alone on the bridge.

A single target comes onto your screen at 12 miles, bearing 030.

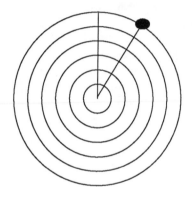

As the Risk of Collision Rule says, you put your bearing marker on the target and watch its progress.

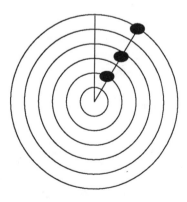

If the target stays on the line or goes off it slightly into your path, there is risk of collision, and you must navigate carefully.

If you see two targets, this won't work, because radars usually have only one bearing marker. There are two ways of dealing with this problem short of full-scale radar plotting.

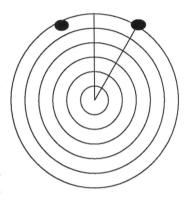

The less satisfactory way is to check the bearings with the bearing marker, write them down on a note-pad, and check them again from time to time.

A better way is to photocopy the radar plotting sheet on the next page. Use a copy machine which can increase the size, and make it as big as will fit on 8½ x 11 paper.

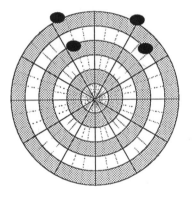

Then check bearings as above, with your radar's bearing marker, and mark on the sheet the position of the targets. A few minutes later, do it again and notice if the targets are staying on the same bearing line.

Keep in mind that you have to take the subsequent bearings of a target when your boat is on the same compass heading, otherwise your boat's yaw can give you false bearings on the targets.

This method doesn't give you as much information as regular rapid radar plotting. You don't get the true course and speed or the relative speed of the target. Thus it would be unsatisfactory for a ship. But boats are more maneuverable and react quicker to the helm and throttles. **Licensed officers and radar observers are still required by the Rules to do full-on rapid-radar plotting.**

Radar Plotting Sheet

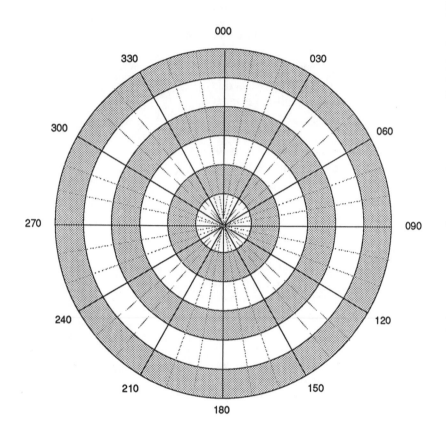

Copy this plotting sheet on a copy machine which can increase the size. Make it as big as will fit on 8½ x 11 paper.

Mark the bearing of a radar target on the plotting sheet. A few minutes later, mark the bearing again, being sure to mark it when your vessel is on the same compass heading.

Keep in mind that a target that changes bearing only slightly can still be a danger of collision.

SECTION 2

Types of Vessels

DEFINITIONS, LIGHTS, DAY SHAPES, RIGHT OF WAY, FOG SIGNALS

This section covers the various types of vessels identified in the Rules of the Road. Each type has a special definiton, its own place in the right-of-way hierarchy, and specific requirements regarding the display of lights and day shapes and the sounding of fog signals.

Lights are the most complicated part of the Rules. Most private boats never use any of them but the running lights and anchor lights, but you need to learn them all so you will know what you are seeing on other vessels. Passing on the wrong wide of a minesweeper or dredge is more dangerous than you want on a Sunday afternoon.

The Rules require three kinds of lights, which tell you

- what direction a vessel is headed (running lights)
- if a vessel is limited in its ability to get out of your way, so the ordinary right-of-way rules have to be adjusted
- if a vessel is doing something which might need your attention

GENERAL REQUIREMENTS FOR LIGHTS

Lights must be shown from sundown to sunrise in any weather. They must also be shown during the day if visibility is restricted by fog, rain, snow, blowing sand, dust, solar eclipse, smoke, or anything else that limits visibility.

You may not show any other light if

- *it can be mistaken for the lights the Rules require*
- *it might impair someone else's ability to see your required lights* (such as decklights next to your running lights)
- *it might interfere with your ability to keep a good lookout* (such as lights on in the wheelhouse)

All except running lights and stern towing lights must be visible from all around the horizon. *(You are allowed a 6-degree blank spot where the mast blocks the light.)*

All-round lights should be shown where best seen, unless otherwise stated, but below the highest masthead light. If more than one light must be shown as a single signal, they must be in a vertical line.

Day Shapes

Boats that have to use special lights at night must show other special signals in the daytime. The day shapes are balls, cones, diamonds, and cylinders, usually strung up in the rigging. The ones you buy in a store are usually nylon on a wire frame that folds flat for storage. *They must be black, and they must be at least 2 feet wide and 2 feet high. A cylinder must be twice as high as it is wide.*

Special Lights

Governments may add special lights or shapes for fishing boats that fish as a fleet. The US doesn't have any special fishing signals.

Governments may also add special lights, shapes, or whistle signals for warships or vessels in convoy. Such special lights may not be of a type that might be confused with regular lights.

RUNNING LIGHTS

To avoid collisions, you have to know what direction other boats are headed. To tell you this, powerboats carry red and green sidelights, a white sternlight, and a white masthead light. Boats over 50 meters (164 feet) have two masthead lights, with the aft one higher than the forward one, so you can know more exactly where it is headed. Sailboats have the same sidelights and sternlight but no masthead light.

Sidelights

Sidelights are red on the port side and green on the starboard.

The way to remember this is that PORT wine is RED.

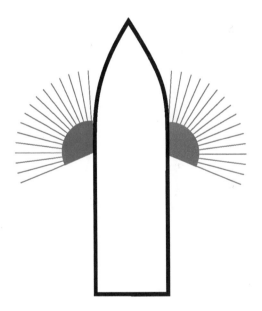

Sidelights must be built or screened so they are visible from straight ahead to 22½ degrees behind the beam, which is a quarter of the way from sideways to straight astern. The screens which direct the light must be painted flat black.

Sidelights are allowed to fade out 3 degrees beyond straight ahead and 5 degrees extra toward the stern.

Masthead Lights

Masthead lights are white. They should be forward of the beam and on the fore-and-aft centerline. They must be visible all around the bow to 22½ degrees abaft the beam, for a total of 225 degrees of arc.

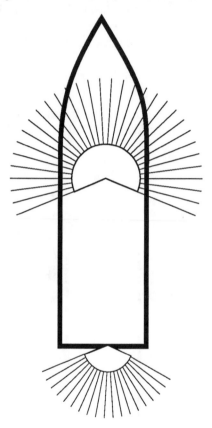

Sternlights

The sternlight points straight astern. It is white and must be visible over 135 degrees of arc. That's three-quarters of the way from astern to abeam on each side.

In theory, the sternlight and masthead lights together make a circle, so you can see one or the other but not both, but lights are allowed to fade out for 5 degrees past the limits, so you will sometimes see both at the same time.

POWER-DRIVEN VESSELS

Right of Way

Power-driven vessels with no special job must stay out of everyone's way except as noted, because they are more maneuverable than other vessels.

Lights

Power-Driven Vessels over 50 Meters (165 Feet)

Sidelights, sternlight, and two masthead lights.

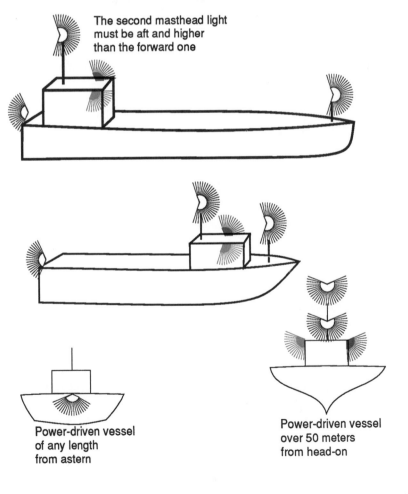

The second masthead light must be aft and higher than the forward one

Power-driven vessel of any length from astern

Power-driven vessel over 50 meters from head-on

Power-Driven Vessels under 50 Meters (165 Feet)

Sidelights, sternlight, and one masthead light.

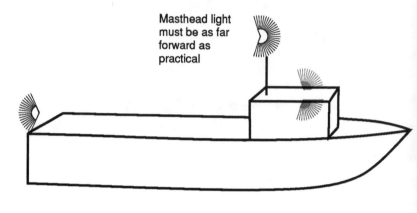

Masthead light
must be as far
forward as
practical

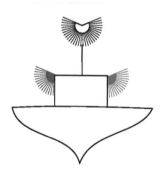

Power-driven vessel
under 50 meters
from head-on

Power-driven vessel
of any length
from astern

Boats under 20 meters (65 feet), in Inland Rules only, do not have to put the masthead light forward of the beam but should have it as far forward as possible.

Power-Driven Vessels under 12 Meters (39 Feet)

Boats under 12 meters may show a single all-round white light instead of the masthead and sternlights.

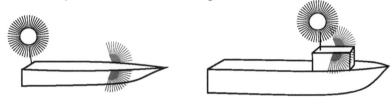

This light may be displaced from the fore-and-aft centerline if necessary, but only if the sidelights are combined in one lantern which is either on the centerline or on the same fore-and-aft line as the white light.

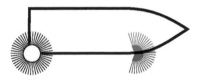

Power-driven boats which both are under 7 meters (23 feet), and whose maximum speed is under 7 knots, may show an all-round white light, with no sidelights. If practical, they should also show sidelights.

This is only in the International Rules. In bays, lakes, and rivers where Inland Rules are in effect, any power-driven boat has to carry sidelights.

In the Great Lakes, a power-driven vessel of any length may substitute one all-round white light for the sternlight and aft masthead lights. This must be carried where the aft masthead light would ordinarily be carried. This light is also permissible in Canadian waters of the Great Lakes.

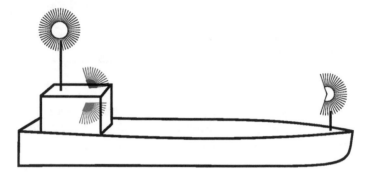

Fog Signals
for any size power-driven vessel underway

'Underway' means any time except when a vessel is at anchor, aground, or made fast to the shore.

When making way,
which means actually moving through the water,   ▬▬▬▬▬
1 long blast every 2 minutes.

When underway but not making way,
which means dead in the water,   ▬▬▬▬ ▬▬▬▬
2 long blasts every 2 minutes.

Long blasts are about 4 seconds long, with about 2 seconds between blasts.

Many loudhailers make an electronic sound at the appropriate interval, so you don't have to keep track of your horn with a stopwatch.

AIR-CUSHION VESSELS

Air cushion vessels include hovercraft and hydrofoils.

Right of Way

For purposes of right-of-way, an air-cushion vessel is the same as an ordinary power-driven vessel.

Lights

When operating in nondisplacement mode (that is, when it is using its hovercraft or hydrofoil capability) it must show an all-round yellow light flashing 120 times a minute . The reason for the yellow light is that air-cushion vessels typically operate at very high speeds, and other vessels need to be warned.

When it is not using its hovercraft capability, an air-cushion vessel must show the ordinary lights for a power-driven vessel.

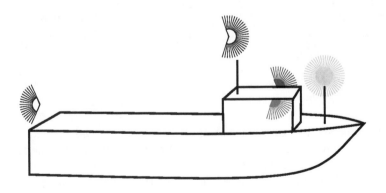

SAILBOATS
Definition

A sailboat is any vessel under sail, as long as it is not using an engine, too. If a sailboat is getting forward motion from a propeller, it is a power-driven boat, even if the sails are up, too.

Right of Way

Sailboats have the right of way over ordinary power boats.

Sailboats must keep out of the way of vessels which are

- *not under command*
- *restricted in ability to maneuver*
- *engaged in fishing*

Sailboats may not impede the safe passage of vessels

- *following a traffic lane*
- *which can safely navigate only in a narrow channel or fairway*

The point of this is clear. Sailboats have the right of way over power-driven vessels because powerboats are more maneuverable. Sailboats do not have the right of way over vessels which are less maneuverable because of their size or jobs.

Sailboats should try not to impede the safe passage of a vessel constrained by its draft.

The category of 'constrained by draft' does not exist in Inland Rules, so this part of the Rule does not apply in American inland waters. Large vessels are unlikely to be constrained by their draft anywhere except in inland waters, so in practice the Rule doesn't mean much in American offshore waters either.

But a vessel constrained by its draft will probably be able to navigate safely only in a narrow channel or fairway, so a sailboat should, according to the previous part of the Rule, not impede its safe passage in inland waters.

Lights

Basic sailboat lights are sidelights and sternlight, but no masthead light.

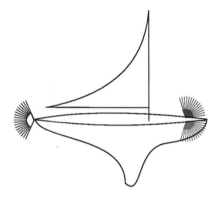

Sailboats under 20 meters (65 feet) may carry a combined lantern at the masthead **instead of** regular running lights, but not in addition to them.

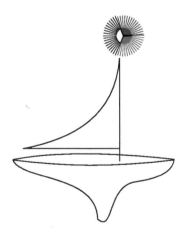

Because sailboats are low in the water, their lights are hard to see, so they may carry extra all-round red over green lights at the masthead. These are in addition to the sidelights and sternlight but not in addition to the combined lantern.

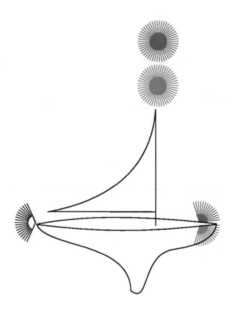

Sailboats under 7 meters (23 feet) *should carry ordinary lights if they can, but may carry instead a flashlight or lantern to show in time to prevent a collision,* usually by shining it on the sail.

Sailboats Using Both Engine and Sails

Any sailboat which is proceeding under sail and at the same time is being propelled by machinery must show lights for a power-driven vessel. During the daytime, a sailboat that is proceeding under sail and power must show a cone, point downward, forward where best seen.

The point of this is that when a sailboat has a motor going, it is more maneuverable than when it is operating only under sail and thus does not deserve the special treatment given sailboats. It is a power-driven vessel, and it must let other boats know that it is one.

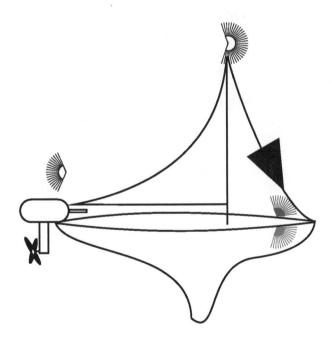

ROWBOATS

Vessels proceeding under oars should carry sidelights and a sternlight.

If this is impractical, they must carry a flashlight or lantern and show it in time to prevent another vessel from hitting them.

LAW ENFORCEMENT VESSELS

In addition to lights of their class, law enforcement vessels may show a flashing blue light when engaged in direct law enforcement activities. This includes federal, state, and local law enforcement vessels.

This is from the Pilot Rules, which apply only in inland waters, but you will see it used in international waters. Law enforcement officers, including the Coast Guard, will expect you to recognize the light anywhere and to obey it. Ignoring a flashing blue light in international waters, while legal, would be very unsafe and would no doubt lead to unpleasantries with the law enforcement officers.

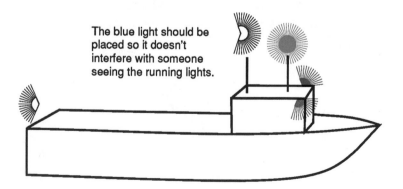

The blue light should be placed so it doesn't interfere with someone seeing the running lights.

VESSELS AT ANCHOR

Lights

Anchor lights are the only all-round lights which may be blocked by more than the mast.

Ships over 100 Meters (328 Feet)

Two all-round white lights, one forward where best seen and one at or near the stern and lower than the forward light.

Ships over 100 meters must also illuminate their decks.

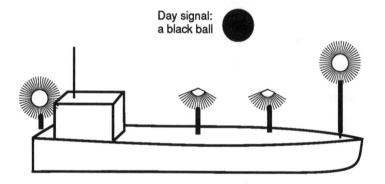

Day signal:
a black ball

Fog Signals

Ring a bell rapidly for 5 seconds every minute in the forepart of the vessel.

Ring a gong for 5 seconds right after the bell in the after part of the ship.

Optional Signal

May sound ▬ ▬▬ ▬ on the horn to warn others of its position.

Boats between 50 and 100 Meters (between 164 and 328 Feet)

The same as vessels over 100 meters except that they don't have to illuminate their decks. Two all-round white lights, one forward where best seen and one at or near the stern and lower than the forward light.

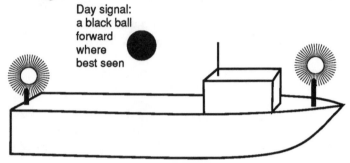

Day signal:
a black ball
forward
where
best seen

Fog Signal

Ring the bell rapidly 5 seconds every minute.

Optional Signal

May sound ▬ ▬▬ ▬ on the horn to warn others of its position

Boats under 50 Meters (164 Feet)

One all-round white light, forward where best seen

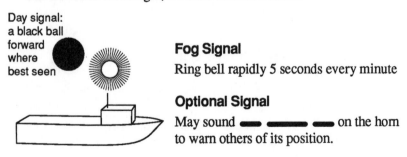

Day signal:
a black ball
forward
where
best seen

Fog Signal

Ring bell rapidly 5 seconds every minute

Optional Signal

May sound ▬ ▬▬ ▬ on the horn to warn others of its position.

Vessels under 20 Meters (65 Feet)

In Inland Rules only, *boats under 20 meters at anchor do not have to show anchor lights if they are anchored in an official anchorage designated by the Secretary of the Treasury.* (In practice, this means the Coast Guard.)

In Inland Rules only, *boats under 20 meters, or barges, canal boats, scows, or other nondescript craft at anchor do not have to ring the bell as a fog signal if they are anchored in an official anchorage designated by the Secretary of the Treasury.*

Boats under 12 Meters (39 Feet)

Boats under 12 meters at anchor must show the same anchor light or shape as larger boats, but they do not have to ring the bell as a fog signal. If they do not, they must make some other efficient sound signal, such as a whistle, siren, or electronic tone, at least once every two minutes.

Boats under 7 Meters (23 Feet)

Boats under 7 meters at anchor do not have to show anchor lights or shapes except when anchored in or near a narrow channel, fairway, or anchorage, or where other vessels normally navigate.

NOT UNDER COMMAND

Definition

Not under command means that the vessel cannot get out of the way of other vessels due to some unusual circumstance.

This means a breakdown of some sort, not a special job.
It is not a distress signal. It has to do with right of way.

Right of Way

A vessel showing not under command has the highest right of way.
It can't avoid you, so you must avoid it.

Lights

A vessel not under command shows two red all-round lights, one over the other. If it is making way, it must add sidelights and sternlight, but not a masthead light.

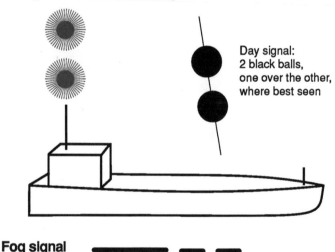

Day signal:
2 black balls,
one over the other,
where best seen

Fog signal ▬▬▬▬ ▬▬ ▬▬

Boats under 12 Meters (39 Feet)

are not required to show not-under-command lights.

AGROUND

Right of Way

A vessel aground has the same right of way as a vessel not under command, since it obviously can't get out of anybody's way.

Lights

A vessel aground is considered to be both anchored and not under command and shows lights for both at the same time.

Ships over 100 Meters (328 Feet)

Two all-round red lights in a vertical line, an all-round white light forward, an all-round white light at or near the stern and lower than the forward white light, and deck illumination.

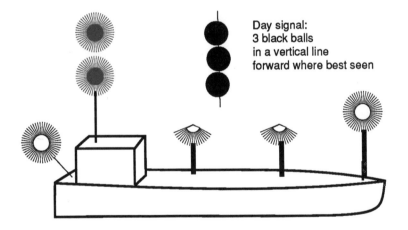

Day signal:
3 black balls
in a vertical line
forward where best seen

Fog Signals

Ring a bell forward for 5 seconds every minute, plus three distinct strokes before and after. Immediately afterward, ring a gong in the after part of the vessel for 5 seconds.

Optional Signal

May sound ━━ ━━━ ━━ on the horn.

Boats between 50 and 100 Meters (between 164 and 328 Feet)

Two all-round red lights in a vertical line, an all-round white light forward, and an all-round white light at or near the stern and lower than the forward white light. This is the same as for larger vessels except that deck illumination isn't required for vessels under 100 meters.

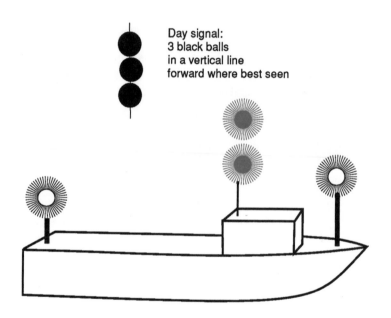

Day signal:
3 black balls
in a vertical line
forward where best seen

Fog Signals

Ring the bell rapidly for 5 seconds every minute,
plus three distinct strokes before and after.

Optional Signal

May sound ▬ ▬▬ ▬ on the horn
to warn others of its position.

Boats under 50 Meters (164 Feet)

Two all-round red lights in a vertical line, where best seen, and an all-round white light, where best seen.

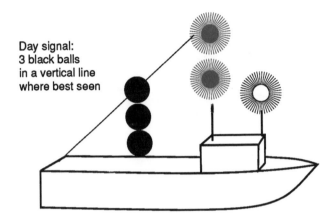

Day signal:
3 black balls
in a vertical line
where best seen

Fog Signals

Ring the bell rapidly for 5 seconds every minute,
plus three distinct strokes before and after.

Optional Signal

May sound ▬▬ ▬▬▬▬▬ ▬▬ on the horn
to warn others of its position.

Boats under 12 Meters (39 Feet)

Must show anchor light or shape but need not show not-under-command lights or shapes. That is, only an all-round white light is necessary.

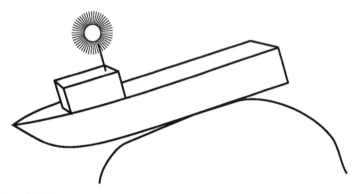

Fog Signals

Boats under 12 meters (39 feet) aground need not ring a bell like the big boats, but if they do not, they must make some other efficient sound signal every two minutes.

Optional Signal

May sound ━ ━━━ ━ on the horn to warn others of its position.

Boats under 7 Meters (23 Feet)

Need not show not-under-command lights or shapes and need not show anchor light or shape unless they are in or near a narrow channel, fairway, or anchorage, or where other vessels normally navigate.

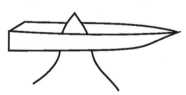

RESTRICTED IN ABILITY TO MANEUVER

Definition

This means a vessel unable to get out of the way due to the nature of its work. This includes but is not limited to:

- *surveying*
- *dredging*
- *laying cable or pipe*
- *servicing navigational marks*
- *launching aircraft*
- *replenishment at sea of persons, provisions, or cargo*
- *towing and unable to change course (add towing lights)*
- *underwater operations, including diving*

This is limited to boats that have jobs to do which make it hard for them to maneuver well enough to get out of the way.

This does not include having a fish on the line, as I once heard it asserted off Cabo San Lucas by a charter-yacht captain chasing a marlin suddenly across a tanker's bow. Having a marlin on the line is fortunate for you but of no interest at all to a tanker on its way to San Pedro.

Right of Way

Vessels restricted in ability to maneuver have the same right of way as those not under command. All other vessels must stay out of the way.

Lights

Red-white-red, all-round lights, in a vertical line. Add running lights for class of vessel.

Day signals: ball-diamond-ball in a vertical line where best seen

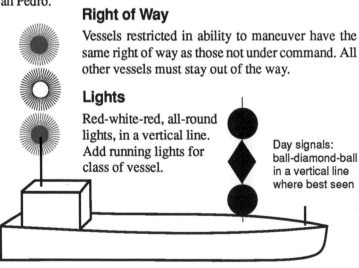

Fog Signal

Vessels Engaged in Underwater Operations (Including Diving)

This is probably the most misunderstood part of the Rules.

Any vessel which is restricted in its ability to maneuver because of dredging or underwater operations at night must show the red-white-red lights for restricted in ability to maneuver.

This is to tell people the vessel can't get out of the way. It has nothing to do with protecting a diver. The Rules have another signal to say a diver is down.

If there is a chance that someone might run over the diver, that is, *if the diver is an obstruction to navigation, or if there is any other obstruction,* such as a buoy, pipeline, stinger, or discharge hose, *then the boat must also show the following signals to point it out:*

On the side of the obstruction
red-over-red
or ball-over-ball

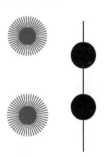

On the side of safe passage
green-over-green
or diamond-over-diamond

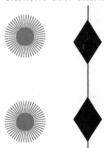

Small Dive Boats

A boat which is engaged in diving but is too small to show the extra lights and shapes on page 46 *may instead show a rigid replica of flag Alpha one meter high and visible all around.*

This is to inform other vessels of an obstruction to navigation. It is **in addition** to the red-white-red lights and **instead of** the regular day shapes (the ball-diamond-ball, ball-over-ball, and diamond-over-diamond).

Flag Alpha

Diver Down

Boats under 12 Meters (39 Feet)

except those engaged in diving operations need not show the red-white-red or ball-diamond-ball for restricted in ability to maneuver.

Dive boats of any size must show the red-white-red lights at night to show they can't get out of the way.

Unofficial Diving Flag

The flag you usually see on dive boats is not from the Rules of the Road. It is a state or local symbol, usually optional and unofficial.

As a flag on a small buoy, it usually means a diver is down in the area.

Dive boats often paint the symbol on the house or fly the flag permanently, so if you see it on a boat, it means only that the boat sometimes engages in diving operations, so you should navigate nearby with caution, paying attention for divers' buoys.

Towboats Restricted in Ability to Maneuver

Towboats that are restricted in their ability to maneuver by their tow may show red-white-red or ball-diamond-ball in addition to the regular towing lights or shapes, which are two or three masthead lights in a vertical line, a yellow towing light over the sternlight, and sidelights.

In practice, many towboats leave their red-white-red up all the time, even when they aren't towing at all, and sometimes at anchor. This is rude and illegal, but there's nothing you can do about it. You have to give them the right of way.

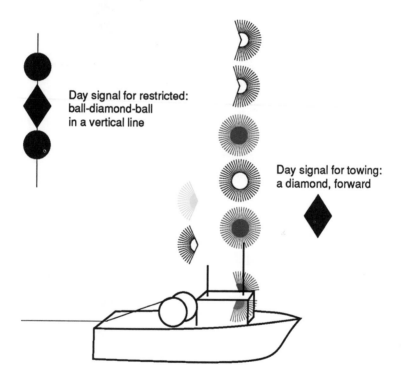

Day signal for restricted:
ball-diamond-ball
in a vertical line

Day signal for towing:
a diamond, forward

Boats Restricted in their Ability to Maneuver when Carrying out their Work at Anchor

Restricted vessels at anchor must add anchor lights or shape, except for vessels engaged in dredging or underwater operations.

Dredges and dive boats do not show anchor lights or shapes.

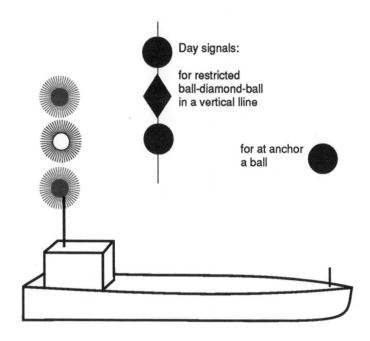

Day signals:

for restricted
ball-diamond-ball
in a vertical lline

for at anchor
a ball

Boats under 12 Meters (39 Feet) except Dive Boats

Boats under 12 meters, except dive boats, need not show the lights or shapes for restricted in ability to maneuver while at anchor.

Dive boats of any size must show the lights or shapes for restricted in ability to maneuver, but not anchor lights.

MINESWEEPERS

Right of Way

Minesweepers are a special class of restricted in ability to maneuver. All other vessels must keep at least 1000 meters away from them.

Lights

Three green lights, one near the foremast head and one at each end of the foreyard, plus regular running lights.

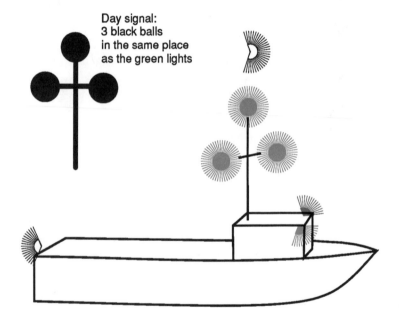

Day signal:
3 black balls
in the same place
as the green lights

If over 50 meters (164 feet), add a second masthead light

If anchored, do not add anchor lights or shape.

VESSELS CONSTRAINED BY THEIR DRAFT

(International Rules Only)

Definition

In the International Rules, *this is a power-driven vessel which is severely restricted in its ability to change course because of its draft compared to the water depth.*

In practice, this will apply mostly to very deep vessels, such as tankers, because it applies only outside inland waters. The Inland Rules do not recognize this class of vessel, so the Rule does not apply on American lakes, rivers, or harbors.

Right of Way

Vessels constrained by their draft must stay out of the way of vessels not under command and vessels restricted in their ability to maneuver by the nature of their jobs.

Other vessels should, if they can, avoid impeding the safe navigation of a vessel constrained by its draft.

Lights

Three all-round red lights in a vertical line, in addition to lights of its class.

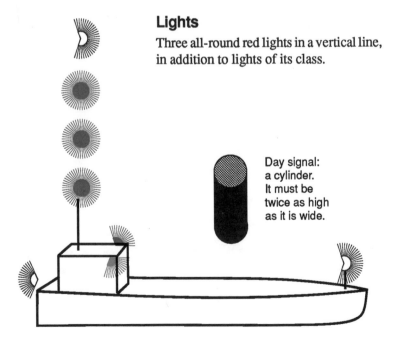

Day signal: a cylinder. It must be twice as high as it is wide.

PILOT BOATS

Right of Way

A pilot boat has no special right of way. It is considered the same as any other power-driven vessel.

Lights

Two all-round lights, white over red, at or near the masthead.
When underway, add sidelights and sternlight but not masthead light.
Vessels over 50 meters (164 feet) add forward masthead light.
At anchor, add anchor lights or shape.
When not on pilotage duty, show only lights of class.

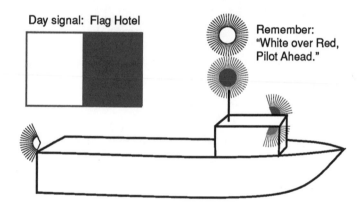

Day signal: Flag Hotel

Remember: "White over Red, Pilot Ahead."

Fog Signals

Ordinary signals for its class
plus morse code letter H (▬ ▬ ▬ ▬)

underway and making way	▬ ▬ ▬ ▬ ▬
underway and not making way	▬ ▬ ▬ ▬ ▬ ▬
at anchor; also ring bell	▬ ▬ ▬ ▬
at anchor, optional; also ring bell	▬ ▬▬▬ ▬ ▬ ▬ ▬
under 12 meters (39 feet)	▬▬▬ ▬ ▬
pilot boat under sail	▬ ▬ ▬ ▬ ▬ ▬

FISHING BOATS

Definition

For the purposes of the Rules, a fishing boat is a boat that is fishing with nets, lines, trawls, or other equipment that makes it hard to get out of your way. **This does not include trolling lines.**

It also does not include fishing boats when they are traveling to or from the fishing grounds, or any time they're not actually doing what it is that restricts their maneuverability.

Right of Way

Fishing boats have the right of way over sailboats and ordinary power boats. Fishing boats must stay out of the way of:

- not under command
- restricted in ability to maneuver
- vessels following a traffic lane

As much as possible, in international waters, fishing boats should stay out of the way of vessels constrained by their draft.

Lights

Two all-round lights, red over white in a vertical line.
Add sidelights and sternlight when underway.
At anchor, show only fishing lights, not anchor lights.

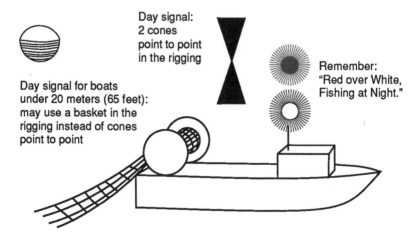

Day signal:
2 cones
point to point
in the rigging

Day signal for boats
under 20 meters (65 feet):
may use a basket in the
rigging instead of cones
point to point

Remember:
"Red over White,
Fishing at Night."

If the fishing boat has gear out over 150 meters (500 feet):
it should show a white light or a cone, with its apex upward, in the
direction of the gear, in addition to the red over white,

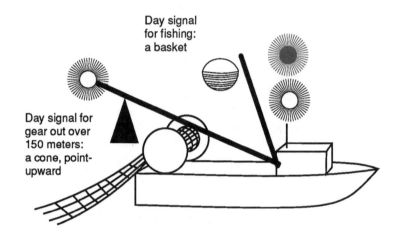

Day signal
for fishing:
a basket

Day signal for
gear out over
150 meters:
a cone, point-
upward

Optional signal for a seiner with its net in the water
alternately flashing yellow lights

Fog Signal   ▬▬▬▬▬   ▬▬   ▬▬

TRAWLERS

Definition

A trawler is a fishing boat dragging a net through the water.

Right of Way

Trawlers have the right of way over sailboats and ordinary power-driven vessels.

They must stay out of the way of vessels which are

- not under command
- restricted in their ability to maneuver,
- following a traffic lane

Lights

Two all-round lights, green over white.

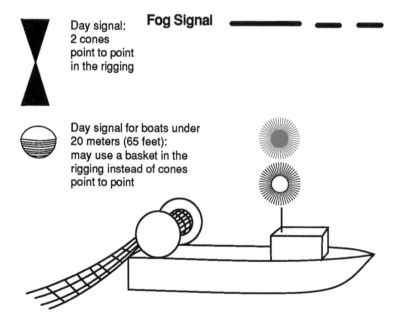

Day signal:
2 cones
point to point
in the rigging

Fog Signal

Day signal for boats under
20 meters (65 feet):
may use a basket in the
rigging instead of cones
point to point

Lights for Trawlers Making Way

If making way, trawlers must add sidelights and sternlight and may add a masthead light, abaft and higher than the green light.

Trawlers over 50 meters (164 feet) making way must add the masthead light abaft and higher than the green light.

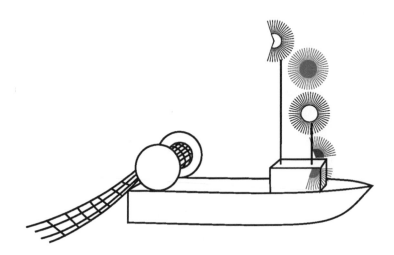

Special Lights

In addition, if trawlers are fishing near other fishing boats, they may show special lights, one over the other, at least 0.9 meters (3 feet) apart and lower than the regular trawling lights.

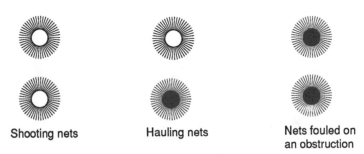

Shooting nets   Hauling nets   Nets fouled on an obstruction

TOWING

Right of Way

For right of way, a towing vessel is considered an ordinary power-driven vessel, unless the tow severely restricts the towboat's ability to change course. If the tow does restrict the towboat's ability to change course, it should show red-white-red for restricted in ability to maneuver.

In practice, some tugs leave all their lights up all the time, so other boats will keep out of their way, or so they don't have to remember to turn them on. I've heard both reasons.

Lights

Pushing ahead, towing alongside, towing astern, and being towed all have different lights and day shapes.

Towing Astern

If the tow is shorter than 200 meters (656 feet) from the stern of the tug to the stern of the tow:
Two masthead lights in a vertical line plus a yellow towing light over the sternlight.

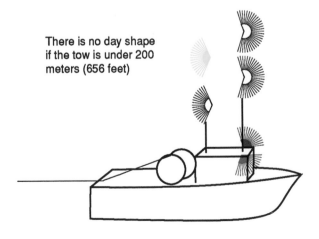

There is no day shape if the tow is under 200 meters (656 feet)

If the tow is over 200 meters (656 feet) from the stern of the tug to the stern of the tow:
Three masthead lights in a vertical line plus a yellow towing light over the sternlight.

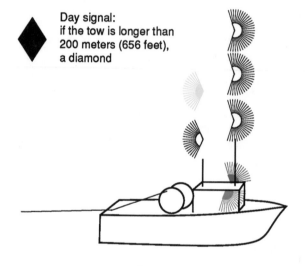

Day signal:
if the tow is longer than
200 meters (656 feet),
a diamond

Fog Signal for Any Towboat

Towed Vessels

Towed vessels carry sidelights and sternlight.

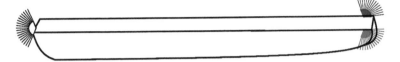

If a towed vessel is 25 meters (82 feet) wide or wider, it must show another white light on each side at the widest point.

If it is over 100 meters (328 feet) long, it must have enough lights that there is no more than 100 meters between lights.

If the tow is inconspicuous or partly submerged, it must show an all-round white light at each end, except that dracones (long, thin tows used in laying pipe) only have to show one at the aft end.

Day Shapes for Towed Vessels

A diamond at the aft end of the tow or the aft end of the last object in the tow. If the two tows are over 200 meters (656 feet), another diamond where best seen and as far forward as possible.

A vessel towed alongside shows the same lights as a stern tow, but no day shape.

Whenever it is impossible to put the proper lights or shapes on a vessel or object being towed, you must do whatever you can to light the tow, or at least to show that it is there. In Inland Rules, this includes shining a searchlight on it.

Fog Signal (only if someone is on board)

▬▬▬▬▬   ▬▬   ▬▬   ▬▬

If possible, sound the fog signal immediately after the tug's signal.

Towing Alongside—International Rules

Two masthead lights in a vertical line, sidelights, and a sternlight, but no yellow towing light.

No day shape.

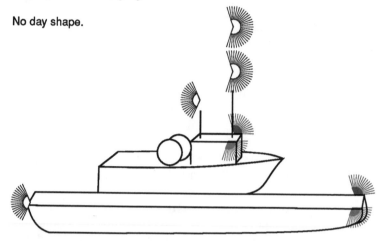

Towing Alongside—Inland Rules

Two masthead lights in a vertical line, sidelights, and two yellow towing lights.

No day shape.

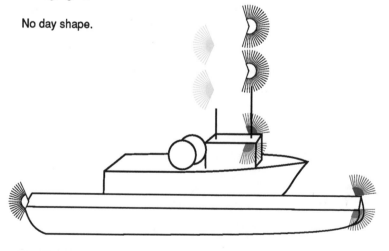

Fog Signal—International or Inland ▬▬ ▬ ▬

Pushing Ahead—International Rules

Pushboat: Two masthead lights in a vertical line, sidelights, and a white stern light. No yellow towing light.

Vessel being pushed: Only sidelights.

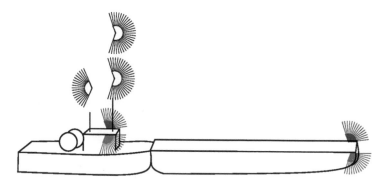

Pushing Ahead—Inland Rules

Pushboat: Two masthead lights in a vertical line, sidelights, and two yellow towing light in place of stern lights.

Vessel being pushed: Sidelights and a special flashing yellow light forward.

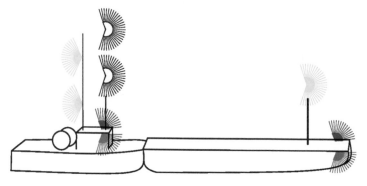

Fog Signal—International and Inland ▬▬▬ ▬ ▬

Pushing Ahead—International and Inland

If a pushboat and the vessel being pushed are rigidly connected, so they handle like a single vessel, they are considered to be a single power-driven vessel for lights and signals.

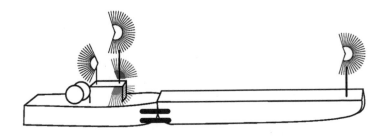

Fog Signal—Underway and Making Way

Fog Signal—Underway but Stopped

Pushing Ahead or Towing Alongside
Special Western Rivers Rule

On western rivers, a boat towing alongside or pushing ahead shows only sidelights and two towing lights astern.

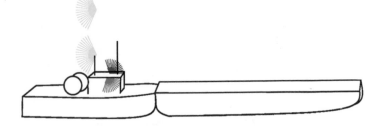

SEAPLANES

Right of way

Seaplanes come dead last for right of way. They must stay out of everybody's way, but if a risk of collision exists, seaplanes must follow the steering rules for a power-driven vessel.

Lights

Seaplanes are also power-driven vessels when it comes to lights.
If a seaplane cannot carry exactly the right lights or shapes, then it must carry as close to them as possible.

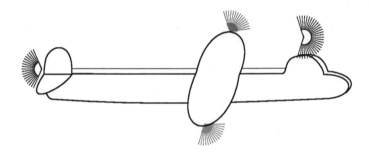

DREDGE PIPELINES

Lighting requirements for dredge pipelines are in the Pilot Rules, which apply in U.S. inland waters.

Dredges with pipelines that are floating or supported on trestles must light the pipeline with a row of yellow lights flashing about once a second. Each end of the pipeline must have red over red.

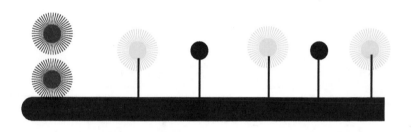

BARGES AT DOCKS OR TIED TO THE BANK

At night, or when the visibility is bad, barges tied up more than two wide or more than 25 meters (82 feet) wide as a group, and any barge that sticks out into a buoyed or restricted channel, or which reduces the available navigable width of a channel to less than 80 meters (262 feet), must show two all-round white lights at the outside corners of the barge or group of barges.

Barges moored in any slip or slough which is used mainly for mooring don't have to show the lights.

THE REAL WORLD

I would be remiss in not warning you that the real world does not correspond exactly to the precise organization of the Rules. Some captains have never heard of the Rules, and some use them to their advantage.

Shrimp boats and fishing boats all over the world have idiosyncratic light systems. In the Bay of Campeche, the lights seem to indicate identity rather than aspect and maneuverability. The locals all know who has the all-round purple over green, or red over orange. A shrimp boat with two all-round white lights on the mast, an all-round green in the aft rigging, and an all-round red in the forward rigging will look like it's headed toward you when it's actually headed to your starboard.

I once almost hit a yacht because the red light over its chart table was brighter than the starboard running light, and I turned the wrong way before seeing the lines of the boat.

Every captain would really prefer that all the other boats kept out of the way. Captains of tugs, dredges, seismic boats, dive boats, and sailboats sometimes carry this to an extreme. This doesn't apply so much to the larger ones, but the smaller tugs seem to leave their red-white-red lights on 24 hours a day just so folks will give them the right of way. I've seen tugs tied to buoys, everyone asleep, with all the running lights, towing lights, red-white-red, and a strobe lit up at once. The captain of a seismic boat once told me, "We leave 'em on all the time, so the other boats leave us alone."

Boats under a hundred tons with scuba divers never show red-white-red or ball-diamond-ball and almost never carry flag alpha. They use the unofficial red flag with a white slash instead, and they leave that one up all the time, so in practice it now tells what a boat does in general rather than what it is doing at that time.

Sailboats not carrying passengers for hire never, repeat *never*, put the cone point-downward in the rigging to indicate that they are running under power and sail at the same time. Sailboaters read the part about powerboats keeping out of their way, but sometimes that seems to be the only part they have read.

Moral: Rule 2. Pay attention, be prepared to wing it, and do what seems safest at the time.

SECTION 3

Steering Rules

The Steering Rules tell who has the right of way when two vessels meet or cross paths, so they don't run into each other. This is the most fundamental part of the Rules. All the lights, shapes, signals and definitions are details to describe who has to stay out of whose way. This section tells how to stay out of the way.

To say one vessel has the right of way over another is a little misleading. When two vessels meet, each has certain duties, and in some ways the duty of the one with the right of way is hardest.

The Basic Rule

In their briefest form, the steering rules say:

If two power-driven vessels are crossing paths, the one coming from the port side must keep out of the way of the one coming from the starboard.

If they meet head on, each should turn a little to starboard.

If one passes another from behind, the one passing must keep clear of the one being passed.

67

Exceptions

There are two general exceptions to the basic steering rules:

First, when one vessel can keep out of the way more easily than another, it should. There are a lot of factors here, including boats under sail, breakdowns, and jobs that restrict maneuverability. You can't just claim that you're not very maneuverable. Categories are precise, and each vessel has to carry particular lights or day shapes to show everyone what category it belongs to. These were discussed in Section 2, Types of Vessels.

Second, in restricted visibility, you might see someone on radar who doesn't see you. You cannot assume someone else's radar is as good as yours. So you must navigate then with special caution and follow special rules.

Running Lights

If you do not already understand basic running lights, go to page 25 first, and then come back here.

RESPONSIBILITIES BETWEEN VESSELS

This rule applies except in narrow channels and traffic separation schemes and when one vessel overtakes another.

Power-Driven Vessels

A power-driven vessel underway must keep out of the way of

- a vessel not under command
- a vessel restricted in its ability to maneuver
- a vessel engaged in fishing
- a sailing vessel

Sailboats

A sailing vessel underway must keep out of the way of

- a vessel not under command
- a vessel restricted in its ability to maneuver
- a vessel engaged in fishing

Fishing Boats

A vessel engaged in fishing when underway, must, as far as possible, keep out of the way of

- a vessel not under command
- a vessel restricted in its ability to maneuver

These all have special definitions within the Rules, which are explained in the Section 2, Types of Vessels, beginning on page 23.

Seaplanes

Seaplanes on the water must generally keep well clear of everyone and avoid impeding their navigation. If a seaplane can't avoid going near boats, it must obey the steering rules for a power-driven vessel.

Vessels Constrained by their Draft

International Rules add that all vessels except those not under command or restricted in their ability to maneuver, must, if they can, avoid impeding the safe navigation of a vessel constrained by its draft. A vessel constrained by its draft must navigate with particular caution, having due regard to its special condition.

Inland Rules don't recognize this category of vessel, but in inland waters it will almost always be a vessel which can safely navigate only in a narrow channel or fairway, so anyone who can should avoid getting in its way.

CROSSING

When two power-driven vessels are crossing, and there is a chance they might run into each other, the vessel on the port side must keep out of the way of the one to starboard. If possible, it should avoid crossing ahead of the other vessel.

The boat on the right has the right of way no matter who gets there first. This Rule applies only if there is risk of collision.

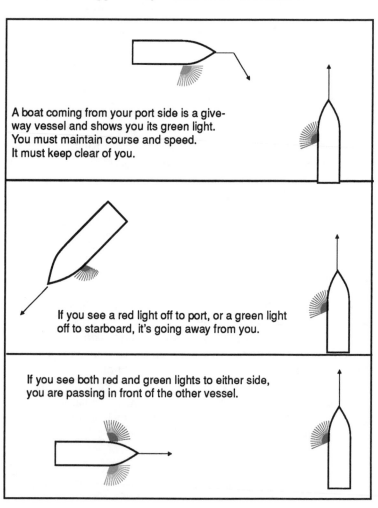

A boat coming from your port side is a give-way vessel and shows you its green light.
You must maintain course and speed.
It must keep clear of you.

If you see a red light off to port, or a green light off to starboard, it's going away from you.

If you see both red and green lights to either side, you are passing in front of the other vessel.

A boat coming from your starboard side shows its red light.
It has the right of way.
It must maintain course and speed.
You must keep clear.

A red light off your starboard bow is a
stand-on vessel crossing in front of you.
it might be coming from any of these
directions.

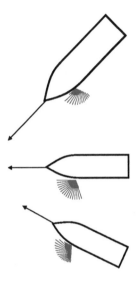

For any of these vessels,
you should turn right, to
pass behind it.

MEETING HEAD-ON

*When two power vessels meet head-on,
so as to involve risk of collision, each
must alter its course to starboard and
pass port to port (red to red).*

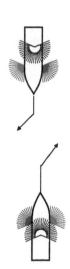

*You must assume there is risk of
collision if at night you would see
both sidelights, or both masthead
lights in a line or nearly in a line.*

*If you have any doubt, you must
assume there is risk of collision and
act accordingly.*

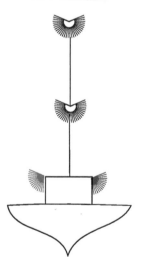

If you see both sidelights,
the boat is within three
degrees of head-on.

If a boat one point off your starboard bow is headed toward you, it's hard to tell if you're meeting or crossing. (1 point is 11¼ degrees. That's an eighth of the way from dead ahead to abeam.)

About 10 degrees off the bow is close enough to call head-on.

If the other captain thinks you're meeting, he will turn to starboard.

If the other captain thinks you're crossing, he will maintain course and speed.

If the other captain is in doubt, he will turn to starboard.

In each case, you should turn to starboard to avoid a collision.

If a boat one point off your port bow is headed this direction, and the other captain thinks you're meeting, he will turn to starboard.

If the other captain thinks you're crossing, he will turn to starboard.

If the other captain has doubt, he will turn to starboard.

You should turn to starboard, too.

OVERTAKING

Definition

The way to distinguish crossing from overtaking is that at night a crossing boat can see your sidelight, but an overtaking boat can see only your sternlight. During the daytime, a vessel is overtaking if at night it would see your sternlight but not your sidelight.

If you see a sidelight ahead, you are a crossing vessel.
If you see only a white light, you are overtaking.

Right of Way

Regardless of anything else in the Rules, any vessel overtaking any other vessel must keep out of the way of the vessel being overtaken.

The vessel being overtaken **always** has the right of way. If a sailboat overtakes a powerboat, the powerboat has the right of way.

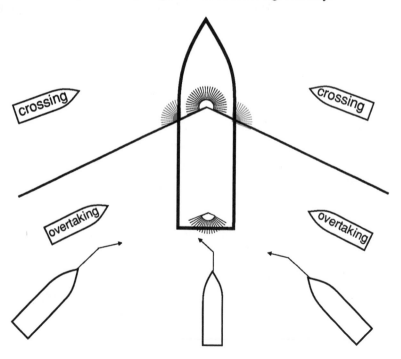

If you can't tell if you are crossing or overtaking, you must assume you are overtaking. (Remember, lights are allowed 5 degrees fade-out.)

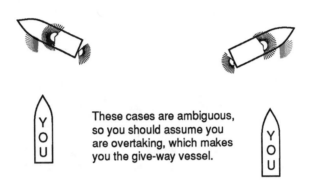

These cases are ambiguous, so you should assume you are overtaking, which makes you the give-way vessel.

If the bearing between you changes, that does not change the overtaker into a crossing vessel. If you start out overtaking, you are overtaking until you are finally past and clear.

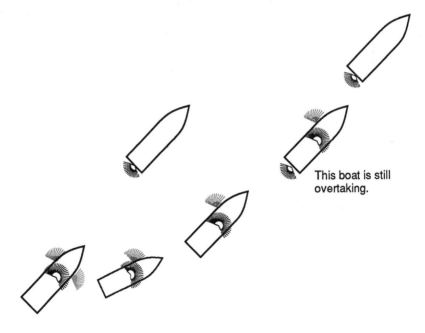

This boat is still overtaking.

ACTION TO AVOID COLLISION

Do it Early

Whatever you do to avoid a collision, you should do it early, so the other vessel doesn't have to guess what you're going to do.

Do it Big

Don't make a series of small changes of course or speed. That just increases the uncertainty of the situation, and uncertainty is what the Rules are trying to get rid of.

The change in course or speed should be big enough that the other captain can see it right away, visually or on radar. It should be early enough and substantial enough to result in passing at a safe distance.

The Rules and the courts tend to define whether you did something right by whether you hit someone or came too close. If you did either, you did it wrong.

Course Change May Be Enough

If you have enough sea room, just changing course might be the best thing to do to avoid coming too close to another vessel, as long as the turn is early enough and big enough, and doesn't put you too close to some other boat.

But sometimes turning isn't enough. *Sometimes you must slow down or stop dead, with your engines in reverse, either to miss someone or to give yourself time to figure out what's happening.*

Stay Alert

You have to keep checking until you're past and clear, taking into account the situation and the requirements of good seamanship.

ACTION BY A GIVE-WAY VESSEL

Whenever the Rules say you must keep out of the way of another vessel, you must, as far as possible, take early and substantial action to keep well clear. This is similar to the Rule on Action to Avoid Collision, on the previous page.

Whatever action you take should be early enough and big enough to be easily seen, and to avoid a close-quarters situation.

ACTION BY STAND-ON VESSEL

If one vessel is required by the Rules to keep out of the way, the other vessel must maintain its course and speed.

This is so the give-way vessel has something predictable to work with. You have to be sensible about this. It doesn't mean that you're forbidden to go about your business whenever you see a ship on the horizon, or that if the channel bends, you have to keep going straight. The steering rules apply only where there is risk of collision. Go about your business unless it would create danger.

Departing from the Rules

*As soon as you see that a boat that is supposed to keep clear of you is not doing so, you **may** do whatever is necessary to avoid hitting it.*

Do What You Have to Do

*If a boat that is supposed to give way comes so close that nothing it can do by itself will be enough to avoid a collision, you **must** do what you can to avoid an accident.*

Try not to Turn to Port

In evading someone who isn't following the Rules, you should try not to turn to port to avoid a vessel on your own port side.

This boat should have turned to
starboard well before this point

If you turn to port and the other boat suddenly turns to starboard, as it should have done earlier, you might run into it head-on, as shown below.

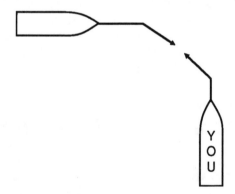

When a vessel doesn't follow the Rules, you don't know what it will do, which is the very thing the Rules were written to prevent.

Instead of turning to port, you can slow down, stop, or turn to starboard.

None of this relieves the give-way vessel of its obligation to keep out of the way.

NARROW CHANNELS

Definition

A narrow channel or fairway is usually a channel of deep water with shallow water on both sides, such as a harbor entrance or a river, or a channel of clear water with obstructions on the side, such as kelp or fish traps. It may or may not be buoyed.

Basic Rule for Narrow Channels

If you are proceeding along a narrow channel or fairway, you should keep as far to the right as safe and practicable.

This is too often ignored, because there are no white lines painted on the water and it's quicker to go straight.

Small Vessels

In International Rules, *a vessel under 20 meters (65 feet) may not impede the passage of a vessel which can safely navigate only in a narrow channel.* This is another case of the more maneuverable staying out of the way of the less maneuverable.

Sailboats

Sailboats also must not impede the passage of a vessel which can safely navigate only in a narrow channel.

Fishing Boats

Fishing boats may not impede the passage of anybody navigating in a narrow channel, regardless of how big or little the boat in the channel is.

Special Rule for Western Rivers and Great Lakes

Inland Rules add one thing here: *On the Western Rivers or Great Lakes, the downriver-bound vessel with a following current has the right of way over an inbound vessel going upcurrent and should give whatever signals are appropriate for the way it intends to pass.*

Crossing a Narrow Channel

No boat may cross a narrow channel if that impedes the passage of a vessel which can't safely navigate outside the channel.

If the vessel going along the channel doubts the intentions of a boat crossing ahead of it, it may sound the danger signal, 5 short blasts.

Anchoring in a Narrow Channel

You should avoid anchoring in a narrow channel if you can.

Horn Signals at Bends in a Channel

If you come to a bend in a narrow channel, or someplace where other boats might be obscured from sight, you must navigate with particular alertness and caution, and you must sound one long blast on your horn, the basic powerboat-underway signal of four to six seconds.

Overtaking in a Narrow Channel

If you overtake someone, especially in a narrow channel or near a shoreline, you should pass on his port side if you can.

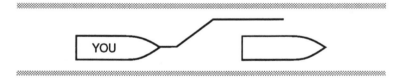

The reason is that if you pass on his starboard side, and he then sees another boat coming head on when you're about halfway past, he's in a scary situation. He's supposed to turn to starboard to avoid a head-on collision, but that would create a collision with you.

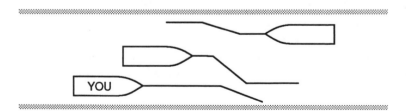

If you are passing to port and the boat you're passing turns to starboard to avoid another boat coming head-on, you can slip back where you were in traffic.

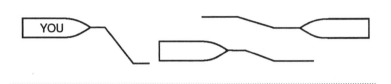

Horn Signals for Overtaking in a Narrow Channel

If you want to pass someone in a narrow channel but can't do it safely unless the boat you want to pass moves over a little, you should sound special horn signals. (These signals aren't used anywhere except in narrow channels.)

If you want to pass on his port side, blow two long and one short.

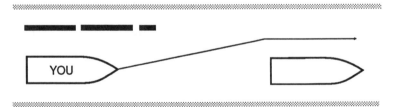

If you want to pass on his starboard side, blow two long and two short.

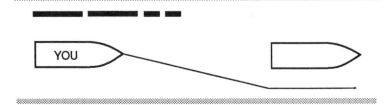

If the other boat agrees, and feels that it is safe, it should answer long-short-long-short and move over to let you by.

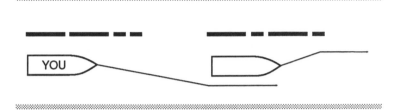

Right of Way during Overtaking

If the boat ahead doesn't understand, or doesn't want to get out of your way, or doesn't think it's safe, you must not try to pass.

The boat being overtaken still has the right of way over a boat that is overtaking it. Always, regardless of any horn signals given.

If the boat ahead doubts that the overtaking boat knows that, *the boat ahead may sound the doubt or danger signal, five short blasts on the horn.*

SHEAR

When vessels pass very close to one another, the water pressure between them can push them apart or pull them together. The water pressure is away from a vessel at the bow and stern and toward it amidships. The force increases with the size and speed of the vessels and decreases with greater distance between them and greater water depth. Large ships can feel the effect when they are as much as 300 meters apart in 60 fathoms of water. Boats passing each other will need to be much closer to feel any effect, but a boat being passed by a large ship can be pushed around easily, and the captain of the boat should be ready to take action to avoid a collision.

When the bow of an overtaking ship passes the stern of a boat, the stern of the boat is pushed away, which pulls its bow toward the ship, increasing the chance of a collision.

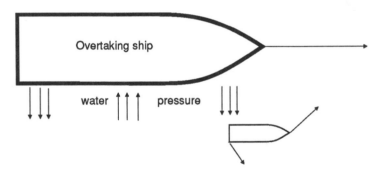

As the ship's bow draws even with the boat's bow, the pressure is reversed, which pushes the boat's bow away from the ship. If the ship is much larger and faster than the boat, this can happen very quickly, and it's possible to lose control.

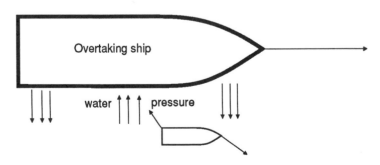

When the ship's stern comes even with the boat's stern, the sterns are pushed apart again, and the bow of the boat is once again drawn in toward the ship.

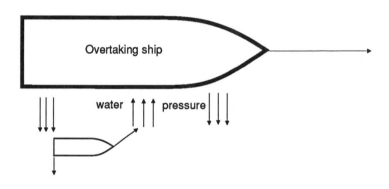

When the ship's stern is even with the boat's bow, the pressures are reversed again.

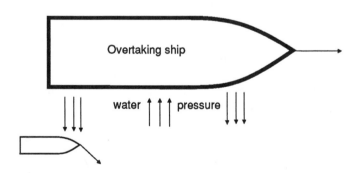

TRAFFIC SEPARATION SCHEMES

In high-traffic areas, the International Maritime Organization sets up traffic separation schemes to reduce the chance of collision by separating ships going one way from ships going the other way. It also separates through traffic from local traffic.

The rules for traffic separation schemes are a lot like the rules for American freeways.

The Basic Rule

You should go the same direction as the other boats in your lane, and keep as far as possible from the center line.

Joining and Crossing a Traffic Lane

You should join a lane at one end or the other, but if you join or leave in the middle, you should merge in or ease out at as small an angle as possible. If you must cross a lane, go straight across.

Who May Use It and Who Must

Ships and large boats must use the traffic lanes rather than the local routes whenever possible, except when going to or from someplace local or to avoid immediate danger.

Sailboats, boats engaged in fishing, and any boat under 20 meters (65 feet) may use the local routes at any time.

If you're not using the traffic lane to get somewhere, stay out of it, and stay as far away from it as you can.

Right of Way

Sailboats and any boat under 20 meters (65 feet) may not impede the safe passage of a power-driven vessel following a traffic lane.

This means you have to know where the lanes are.

Anchoring in a Traffic Lane

Don't anchor in a traffic lane unless you absolutely must, or near where a lane ends or starts. There's a lot of traffic there, and it's going every which way.

Separation Zones

The only vessels that may go into a separation zone are

- *fishing boats*
- *boats crossing the lanes*
- *boats that must do so to avoid immediate danger*
- *boats laying or servicing a submarine cable*
- *boats engaged in an operation for the maintenance of safety of navigation*

Fishing boats may fish in the separation zone between the lanes, but they may not impede the passage of any vessel following the traffic lane.

Remember: Fishing boat has a specialized meaning in the Rules. It does not include fishing with rod and reel or trolling lines.

Vessels Entirely Exempt from this Rule

Boats laying or servicing submarine cable or engaged in operations for the maintenance of safety of navigation are exempt from anything in this Rule to the extent that it is necessary for them to do their jobs.

Seismic vessels, which tow electronic noisemakers on two miles of tow-line to find oil, have to go in straight lines for miles and miles at a time. They tow a cable, but they don't *lay* cable or engage in operations for the maintenance of safety of navigation, so they are not entitled to the exemption. They do, however, claim it, and sometimes they go the wrong way in a busy traffic lane, so be ready to dodge them, and remember to use good radio manners when you explain the Rule to the seismic vessel. The poor captain is just going where his surveyors told him to go and doesn't like it any more than you do.

CONDUCT OF VESSELS IN RESTRICTED VISIBILITY
Definition

The basic steering rules say what boats must do when they meet in clear weather, so each captain knows what the other will do. *This Rule applies to vessels who don't see each other visually when navigating in or near an area of restricted visibility.*

Restricted visibility includes fog, smoke, blowing sand, dust, rain, and snow. It also covers situations in which you might be in clear weather, but with a squall or fog bank nearby. If you see another vessel only on radar, it might not see you. Even if you don't see any vessels on radar, one might still be hidden in a squall, so you have to act as though one is there.

Requirements of Good Seamanship

The Rule reminds us of some points already covered in other Rules:

You must travel at a safe speed, bearing in mind that you can't see very well.

In following the Rules on lookout, safe speed, risk of collision, action to avoid collision, narrow channels, traffic separation schemes, and good seamanship, you must take into account the situation at the time, including how good the visibility is.

If you see someone on radar but not visually, you must determine if there is risk of collision and whether you might come too close.

If there is any risk of collision, or of coming too close, you must do something early enough to avoid it.

A power-driven vessel must have its engines ready for immediate maneuver. This is mainly for ships, which change speeds in the engine room rather than on the bridge.

Do not Turn to Port for a Vessel forward of the Beam

If you change course to avoid hitting someone, as far as possible, avoid turning to port for a target forward of the beam, except when you are overtaking it. Otherwise you might run into it if it's headed in certain directions.

If you see these targets on a radar screen, they might be these boats.

or

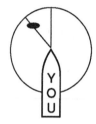 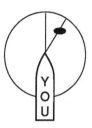

You don't know if they see you.
They don't know if you see them, either.

If they turn, it will be to starboard, because you are forward of their beam.

If you turn, it should be to starboard, too, because they're forward of your beam. If you turn to port, as shown, you might run right into them.

Do not Turn toward a Vessel abeam or abaft the Beam

As far as possible, you should also avoid turning toward a vessel beside you or behind you, abeam or abaft the beam.

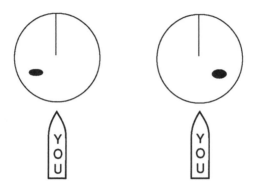

The radar screens above could indicate these two boats behind you, intending to pass.

If you turn toward them, they might run into you.

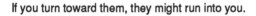

Hearing a Fog Signal forward of the Beam

Unless you have determined that there is no risk of collision, if you hear a fog signal of someone apparently forward of your beam, or if you can't avoid coming close to someone forward of your beam, you must slow to bare steerageway, the minimum at which your boat can stay on course. On boats, this means engines in gear, throttles back.

If necessary, you must take all way off (stop all propulsion, engines out of gear or even in reverse, to stop completely). *In any case, you must navigate with extreme caution until the danger of collision is over.*

STEERING RULES FOR SAILBOATS

Definition

A sailboat is a vessel which is propelled by sails alone. If it gets any propulsion from a motor or engine, it is a power-driven vessel for the purposes of the Rules.

Right of Way over Powerboats

In general, if a powerboat meets a sailboat, the powerboat keeps out of the way of the sailboat.

Exceptions

A sailboat must keep out of a powerboat's way if the sailboat is overtaking the powerboat, or if the powerboat

- can navigate safely only in a narrow channel
- is in a vessel traffic lane
- is not under command
- is restricted in its ability to maneuver
- is fishing, or trawling
- is towing something which severely restricts its ability to change course

The reason for these exceptions is that in these cases, the sailboat is more maneuverable than the powerboat.

Two Sailboats Approaching One Another

When two sailboats are approaching one another, and there is a chance they might collide, if they have the wind on different sides, the boat with the wind on the port side must keep clear of the other.

If they both have the wind on the same side, the upwind boat must keep clear of the downwind boat.

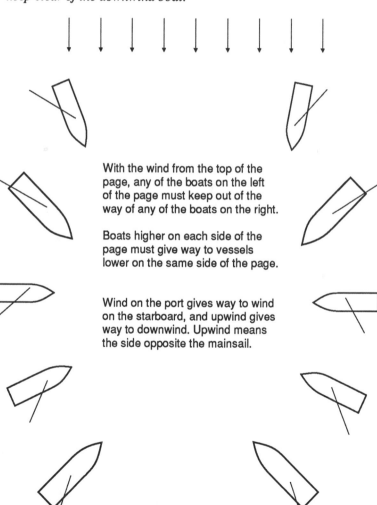

With the wind from the top of the page, any of the boats on the left of the page must keep out of the way of any of the boats on the right.

Boats higher on each side of the page must give way to vessels lower on the same side of the page.

Wind on the port gives way to wind on the starboard, and upwind gives way to downwind. Upwind means the side opposite the mainsail.

If a sailboat with the wind on its port side sees a sailboat upwind of it, but it can't tell which side the second boat has the wind on, it must keep out of the way.

This is because if the other boat has the wind on its starboard side, it will be expecting the first boat to give way.

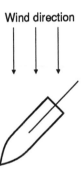

Stand-on vessel

Give-way vessel

SECTION 4

Signals

General Requirements

Every boat 12 meters (39 feet) or longer must have a horn.
Boats shorter than 12 meters do not have to have a horn, but must have some means of making an efficient sound signal, such as a whistle, siren, or electronic tone.

The Length of a Blast on the Horn

A short blast on a horn is about one second.
A long blast is 4 to 6 seconds.
A series of blasts should have about one second between them.

A Note on the Language

The Rules actually call a long blast "prolonged." They do this because Inland Rules used to require 3 kinds of blast, so they needed 3 different words for 3 blast lengths.

A "short" blast was 1 second long.
A "prolonged" blast was 4 to 6 seconds long.
A "long" blast was 8 seconds long.

But the Inland Rules were reformed. There is no longer an 8-second blast, so there is no reason for 3 different words.

"Long" and "short" sound better than "prolonged" and "short."

The Rules call the horn a whistle. They define it as anything that can make the right sound, which is described by decibel and wavelength in Annex III, if you should ever want to build a horn.

Most boats use a horn to make that sound, so I call a whistle a horn, which I define as anything that will make the right sound.

To run a boat, all you need to know about horns is that a horn has to be within a certain range of tones and has to be loud enough to be heard by another vessel.

MANEUVERING SIGNALS

This rule applies only to power-driven vessels.

The Basic Rule

Whenever a power-driven vessel underway is required or permitted by the Rules to maneuver while in sight of another vessel (not just in sight of power-driven vessels), *it must blow its horn*

1 time for changing course to starboard ➡

⬅ ⬅ *2 times for changing course to port*

3 times for engines going astern.

Inland Rules: Same Signal, Different Meaning

In the Inland Rules, the same signals mean "I **intend** to turn," and you must wait for an identical answering signal before you can begin your turn.

Danger or Doubt

If you are approaching another vessel in sight of one another, and you fail to understand its intentions or actions, or if you doubt that the other vessel is taking enough action to avoid a collision, you should sound at least 5 short and rapid blasts to show your doubt.

▬ ▬ ▬ ▬ ▬

Maneuvering Light

If you want to, you may flash a light at the same time you blow the horn for maneuvering signals. The signal should be one second per flash, one second between flashes, and at least ten seconds between signals.

1 flash for changing course to starboard,
2 flashes for changing course to port,
3 flashes for engines going astern.

The maneuvering light is only for changing course, going astern, or in case of doubt. *It must be all-round white, on the same fore-and-aft line as the masthead light, within 2 meters above or below the masthead light.* Inland Rules allow white or yellow.

Passing in Narrow Channels

If you want to overtake someone in a narrow channel, and you want the other boat to move over, to make it safe,

you should blow ▬▬ ▬▬ ▬
for "I intend to pass on your starboard side"

or ▬▬ ▬▬ ▬ ▬
for "I intend to pass on your port side."

If the vessel to be overtaken agrees to be overtaken, it should sound ▬▬ ▬ ▬▬ ▬

If not, it should sound the doubt signal, ▬ ▬ ▬ ▬ ▬

Approaching a Bend in a Channel

If you get near a bend in a channel or someplace where other vessels may be hidden from view, sound one long blast.   ▬▬▬▬

If a boat hears you from the other side of the obstruction, it should answer with one long blast.   ▬▬▬▬

Horn Signals in the World of Small Boats

The Rule requiring horn signals for changes of course was written for ships and before radios.

It was not expected by the framers of this Rule that yachts in Newport Harbor would always give horn signals before making a turn. If you tried to use passing signals there, no one would know what you meant, but you might hear a lot of random horn blowing in return.

In the real world, freighters, tankers and other ships give horn signals, but you almost never hear them from boats, even from boats requiring licensed officers.

That is partly due to the radio. VHF Channel 13 is reserved for calling bridge-to-bridge to discuss matters concerning navigation, such as intentions to turn or keep on course. Ships usually make their intentions known to each other that way or on Channel 16.

SOUND SIGNALS IN RESTRICTED VISIBILITY
Application
This rule applies in or near an area of restricted visibility, including in clear weather near a fog bank or a squall.

Basic Powerboat Signals ▬▬▬▬▬
A power-driven boat making way through the water must sound one long blast on the horn (that's 4 to 6 seconds) *every two minutes.*

Loud hailers often have an automatic electronic horn built in.

Vessels Limited in Maneuverability ▬▬▬ ▬ ▬
Vessels limited in their maneuverability must sound one long and two short blasts on the horn every two minutes.

This includes not under command, sailboats, fishing boats, restricted in ability to maneuver, and towing or pushing, unless the tow and push are rigidly connected.

Vessels being Towed   ▬▬▬▬ ▬ ▬ ▬
A vessel being towed, or the last one in the tow, must blow one long and three short blasts on the horn every two minutes if anyone is aboard. If practical, this should be done immediately after the signal given by the towboat.

Vessels at Anchor   ▬ ▬▬▬▬ ▬
A vessel at anchor must ring a bell rapidly for 5 seconds every minute in the forepart of the vessel.
*   A vessel at anchor may also sound short-long-short on the horn to warn other vessels of its position.*

A vessel over 100 meters (328 feet) at anchor *must ring a bell rapidly for 5 seconds every minute in the forepart of the vessel and then ring a gong rapidly for 5 seconds in the after part of the vessel.*

Fishing Boats and Vessels Restricted in their Maneuverability at Anchor ▬▬▬ ▬ ▬

Fishing boats, when fishing at anchor, and vessels restricted in their ability to maneuver, when doing their work while at anchor, blow the limited maneuverability signal, one long and two short, every two minutes, instead of the anchor signal.

Vessels Aground ▬ ▬▬ ▬

A vessel aground sounds the anchor bell signal plus three separate and distinct strokes of the bell before and after the rapid ringing of the bell. A vessel aground may also sound short-long-short on the horn.

Vessels under 12 Meters (39 Feet)

Vessels under 12 meters (39 feet) are not required to give these signals, but if they don't, they must make some other big noise at least once every two minutes.

Pilot Boats ▬ ▬ ▬ ▬

A pilot boat, while on pilot duty, may blow four short blasts in addition to the regular signals of its class as an identity signal.

Inland Rules Exemptions

Inland Rules add that

- *boats under 20 meters (65 feet)*
- *barges*
- *canal boats*
- *scows*
- *other non-descript craft*

do not have to make the anchor signals if they are anchored in a special anchorage area designated by the Coast Guard.

FOG SIGNALS

Long blast — 4 to 6 seconds ▬▬▬▬

Short blast — 1 second ▬

▬▬▬ Power-driven vessel underway

▬▬▬ ▬▬▬ Power-driven vessel underway but stopped, not making way

▬▬▬ ▬ ▬ Not under command

▬▬▬ ▬ ▬ Restricted in Ability to Maneuver even when at anchor

▬▬▬ ▬ ▬ Constrained by draft (international only)

▬▬▬ ▬ ▬ Sailboats

▬▬▬ ▬ ▬ Fishing boats, even when at anchor

▬▬▬ ▬ ▬ Towing or pushing ahead

▬▬▬ ▬ ▬ ▬ Vessel being towed

▬ ▬ ▬ ▬ Pilot vessel add underway or anchor signals

▬▬▬ ▬ ▬▬▬ Anchored (optional)

BELL SIGNALS

Anchored : Ring a bell rapidly for 5 seconds every minute.

Anchored over 100 meters (328 feet): Add a gong aft , after the bell.

Aground: Add three separate and distinct hits on the bell before and after ringing the bell.

A boat under 12 meters does not have to sound the usual horn signals but must have some other 'efficient sound signal' and use it every 2 minutes.

Inland Rules only: A barge, scow or other non-descript vessel, or a vessel under 20 meters, doesn't have to give the signal for at anchor if it is anchored in a specially designated anchorage.

DISTRESS SIGNALS

When a vessel is in distress and needs help, it should use or show any of the following signals:

- Red star shells
- Red parachute flare
- Continuous sounding of the fog horn
- Flames on the vessel; obviously this is dangerous in itself and should only be done if it can be done reasonably safely, such as making the flames in a barrel
- Gun fired at intervals of one minute
- Distress flag with a black ball and square on an orange background
- Anything square over anything round in the rigging or on the mast, such as a flag over an anchor ball
- Code flag November over code flag Charlie
- Any color dye marker
- Smoke flare
- SOS by radio telegraph or by light signal
- Mayday by radio

▬ ▬ ▬   ▬ ▬ ▬ ▬ ▬   ▬ ▬ ▬

- Radio-telegraph alarm
- Radio-telephone alarm
- Emergency Position Indicating Radio Beacon (EPIRB)
- Wave your arms

Limitations on the Use of Distress Signals

You must not use any distress signal unless you are in distress.
I once saw a distress flag (orange flag with a black square and ball) used by a 105-foot sportfishing boat with three licensed operators aboard to mark a fishing spot off the coast of Baja California .

You must not use any other signal that might be confused with a distress signal.

Strobe Lights in Inland Rules

In addition to the International list, the Inland Rules add one distress signal which the International Rules forbid, the strobe light, a high-intensity white light flashing at regular intervals from 50 to 70 times a minute.

The International Rule on the next page specifies that a strobe light should not be used to attract attention because it might be mistaken for a buoy or other aid to navigation. You have enough unambiguous signals without having your distress signal mistaken for a harbor entrance or a gill net.

SIGNALS TO ATTRACT ATTENTION

The Basic Rule

You may make other signals to get a vessel's attention, as long as these signals can't be mistaken for any other signal in the Rules.

Searchlights

You may shine your searchlight in the direction of danger, as long as you don't cause anybody any problems with it. (There's nothing scarier than having a supply boat under an oil rig and being blinded by a searchlight.)

Restrictions

You can't use any light to get someone's attention if it might be mistaken for an aid to navigation, such as a buoy.

Strobes

You may not use strobe lights and other high intensity intermittent or revolving lights. Someone might think the light is on a navigation buoy and run into trouble.

As stated on page 102, the Inland Rules specifically allow strobe lights as a distress signal, while the International Rules say they should never be used to attract attention. This is the most direct contradiction between the International and Inland Rules.

In practice, the strobes you see offshore are usually on commercial fishing boats, shut down for the night with everyone asleep, to avoid being hit by freighters or sportfishers.

SECTION 5

Penalties for Violations

I said in the introduction that the Rules have the force of American law for any vessel in U.S. waters and for any American vessel anywhere in international waters. They really mean it when they say 'force' of law.

VIOLATIONS OF
INTERNATIONAL RULES OF THE ROAD

The Basic Penalty

Any person who is supposed to follow the Rules, but doesn't, can be fined up to $5000 for each violation. Any vessel that is supposed to follow the rules, but doesn't, can be fined up to $5000 for each violation.

Technically, this could include a burned-out running light. It would be very unlikely, but it could happen. The Coast Guard gets funny sometimes.

If You Can't Pay

If the owner doesn't have the money, the government can take the boat instead. If you still can't or don't pay your fine, the Secretary of Transportation may ask the Attorney General to go after you in court, no matter how small the amount of money, and do to you whatever the law says they can do.

Who Has the Power

The Secretary of Transportation may impose these fines, or any other civil penalty the laws allow, or may reduce or waive any penalty. If the Coast Guard switches cabinet departments, the secretary of the new department gets to impose the penalties.

Requirement for Notice

Nothing can be done to anyone before giving them notice of the violation and the opportunity for a hearing.

VIOLATIONS OF
INLAND RULES OF THE ROAD

The penalties for violating Inland Rules are the same as for violating the International Rules ($5000 per violation).

In addition, if a foreign vessel doesn't pay a fine or do whatever it has been told to do, the Secretary of Transportation may withhold or revoke its clearance to come into the U.S. The vessel might be allowed to enter after posting a bond.

DUTY OF THE MASTER IN A COLLISION
You Must Give Help

If you are in charge when your boat and another boat collide, you must do what you can and whatever is necessary to save the other boat from any danger caused by the collision, unless it would put your own boat, crew, or passengers in serious danger. And you must stay by the other boat until you are sure it needs no more help, unless that would put you in serious danger.

You Must Give Information

You must tell the other captain

- *the name of your boat*
- *your home port*
- *where you're coming from*
- *where you're going*

If you don't, the collision will be declared to be your fault unless you come up with reasonable cause for not stopping or proof that the collision wasn't your fault.

Penalties

Neglecting any of these duties is a misdemeanor worth $1000 or two years in jail. If you don't have the money, the government can take your boat.

Half of the money goes to the Treasury, and the other half goes to the informer. Honest. It's right there in the law.

FEDERAL BOAT SAFETY ACT OF 1971

Negligence

The penalty for using a vessel in a negligent manner so as to endanger the life, limb, or property of any person is $500 per violation.

A gross violation can cost $1000 and/or a year in jail. The Coast Guard would without doubt consider causing a collision while using alcohol or drugs to be a gross violation.

Requirement to Give Assistance

If you are involved in a collision, you must give all practical and necessary assistance, without putting yourself into serious danger.

Good Faith Efforts to Help

If you help in good faith and act as an ordinary, reasonably prudent person would have acted in the same or similar circumstances, you cannot be held liable for any civil damages as a result of your helping or for any act or omission in providing or arranging salvage, towage, medical treatment, or other assistance.

SECTION 6

Summary of Rules for Boats Under 20 Meters (65 feet)

Narrow Channels

Boats shorter than 20 meters long may not impede the passage of vessels which can safely navigate only in a narrow channel.

Traffic Lanes

Boats shorter than 20 meters may not impede the passage of power-driven vessels following a traffic lane, but they may use the inshore traffic lanes at any time.

Sailboat Running Lights

Sailboats under 20 meters may combine their running lights in one lantern carried at or near the top of the mast. This is instead of regular running lights, not in addition to them.

Fishing Boat Day Shapes

Fishing boats under 20 meters may use a basket for a day shape instead of two cones point to point. The same is true of trawlers.

Inland Rules for Anchorages

In the Inland Rules only, a vessel under 20 meters doesn't have to show anchor lights or shapes when anchored in special anchorages designated by the Coast Guard.

In the Inland Rules only, a vessel under 20 meters doesn't have to sound the at-anchor fog-horn signal when anchored in special anchorages designated by the Coast Guard.

BOATS UNDER 12 METERS (39 FEET)

Horn Signals

Boats shorter than 12 meters don't have to have a horn, but must have some way of making an efficient sound signal. They don't have to have a bell and don't have to give the anchor bell-signals, but must make some other efficient sound signal at least once every 2 minutes.

Masthead and Stern Lights

Boats shorter than 12 meters may use an all-round white light instead of the masthead and stern lights.

The Inland Rules let it go at that and don't say where the light has to go. The International Rules say you can move it off the fore-and-aft centerline if you have to, provided the running lights are combined in one lantern, which is on the fore-and-aft centerline, or as near as possible to the fore-and-aft line of the all-round white light.

Aground Lights

Boats under 12 meters don't have to show red-over-red or three balls in a line to signal that they are aground but they must still show anchor signals, unless they are in a special anchorage designated by the Coast Guard.

Restricted in Maneuverability Lights

Boats shorter than 12 meters, except for dive boats, do not have to show red-white-red or ball-diamond-ball for restricted in ability to maneuver.

Requirement to Carry Rules

The Pilot Rules require that the operator of any self-propelled vessel longer than 12 meters must carry a copy of the Inland Rules on board and maintain them for ready reference.

BOATS UNDER 7 METERS (23 FEET)

Running Lights

Boats shorter than 7 meters and whose maximum speed is not more than 7 knots may show an all-round white light instead of the stern and bow lights, and should show sidelights if possible.

Restricted in Maneuverability Lights

Boats shorter than 7 meters don't have to show red-white-red or ball-diamond-ball for restricted in ability to maneuver, even if it's a dive boat. This is International Rules only.

Anchor Lights

Boats shorter than 7 meters don't have to show anchor lights or shapes unless they are in or near a narrow channel, fairway, or anchorage, or where other boats normally navigate.

Sailboat Running Lights

Sailboats shorter than 7 meters must show running lights if possible, but if they can't, they must have a flashlight or lighted lantern ready at hand to show in sufficient time to prevent collision.

Also by Michael Cargal

C^THE_aptain's Guide
Life^TO_raft
Survival (CAPTAIN CARGAL MICHAEL)

If you are already in a liferaft,
do the following in this order.
① Get everybody out of the water
② Cut loose from the sinking vessel
③ Deploy the sea anchor
(SOME ARE AUTOMATIC)
④ Treat serious injuries (SEE PAGE 15)
⑤ Prevent exposure (SEE PAGE 19)
⑥ Take inventory
⑦ Call for help
⑧ Read the rest of this book

200 pp. illustrated 1990

"A good book and recommended for your raft's package."
American Sailor

"Enjoyable and very well written ... a really good book."
Hudson River Boating News

SHERIDAN HOUSE